MORE FROM A BOOK

CU00661482

Presenting Design Work
Donna Spencer

Practical Pair Programming
Jason Garber

Writing for Designers
Scott Kubie

Image Performance
Mat Marquis

Webfont Handbook
Bram Stein

Animation at Work
Rachel Nabors

Color Accessibility Workflows
Geri Coady

Making Sense of Color Management
Craig Hockenberry

Working the Command Line
Remy Sharp

Visit abookapart.com for our full list of titles.

Publisher: Jeffrey Zeldman
Designer: Jason Santa Maria
Executive director: Katel LeDû
Managing editor: Lisa Maria Marquis
Editors: Sally Kerrigan, Chris Hagge, Caren Litherland
Book producer: Ron Bilodeau

ISBN: 978-1-952616-06-8

A Book Apart
New York, New York
http://abookapart.com

TABLE OF CONTENTS

For Minnie and Eva, my great-grandmother and great-aunt. Lifelong (and long-lived) readers, writers, teachers, and beacons of good cheer.

FOREWORD

HI, CONTENT FRIEND.

Beth invited me to write three-hundred words for this book foreword. That's an Instagram caption, really. At least for a writer like me, who always seeks to capture nuance and impart gravitas.

So just three-hundred words? Well, that doesn't seem quite enough to set the stage, especially for such an important book as this.

The pressure. She's on.

Let's hop to it. Just as Beth did when, a mere few paragraphs into this book, she articulates perfectly the tension so many of us feel as content strategists, producers, designers.

We love our jobs. We believe in content's ability to transform organizations. Yet we aren't seen as strategic partners. Too often we get the directive: "Just give me three-hundred words." Or: "Can you just make this sound better?"

No one scoots over to make room for us at the Table of Strategic Decision-Making; no one views as more than grammar geeks. (Also: Everyone qualifies an ask with "just." Annoying.)

As Beth puts it: "You're always frosting a really terrible cake, but you don't know how to get your hands on the recipe book—how to change the way content works in your organization."

So that's what Beth does here. And beautifully.

Beth doesn't just tell you about the tools you'll need (the cake pan, the mixing bowl, and the measurements, in this analogy). She gives you the power to fundamentally change your organization's approach to content. She gives you the recipe, the raw ingredients, and the entire kitchen, complete with a Viking range and hood (the 48-inch professional-series model).

Beth also offers tactical ideas to truly bake in (LOL) your position as a strategic content lead—giving you newfound respect, influence, esteem, reverence, support, appreciation, access...plus a squad of sous chefs and a finer crumb on your cake. And a tighter butt.

Just kidding on that last one. Maybe.

In my own work, I seek to empower content creators and strategists to do work that matters. You already do work that matters—so this is your opportunity to get your entire organization to understand your worth.

Now you can have your cake. And everyone else gets to eat it, too.

—Ann Handley

INTRODUCTION

THIS IS NOT A BOOK ABOUT how to do content design. It's not about how to write error messages, blog posts, website pages, or onboarding guides. It isn't even about how to do the research, discovery, and exploration necessary before all the writing begins.

You probably already know how to do all those wonderful things. And if you don't, or you need a refresher, there are some truly superb books, courses, and conferences out there that cover these topics in loving detail. You can check them out anytime—but please don't take them for granted. Not too long ago, you'd have been seriously hard-pressed to find high-quality resources that focused on content design as a fully fledged discipline. It wasn't that long ago that it was just as difficult to find other practitioners working on content design as their full-time job.

But in the past decade or so, all that has changed. Content design is *everywhere* now. It's a term people in very different disciplines throw around with abandon. And it has never been easier to learn the fundamentals of content design, content strategy, and user experience (UX) writing, or to find a job that requires these skills.

And yet.

Even now that we have a bookshelf full of books, now that we have content design courses we can take online or at a handful of accredited schools, now that we're surrounded and supported by a global community of like-minded friends, content designers still struggle to drive visible impact, influence strategy, and drill down to the real core of what content can do.

Some of this is perfectly fair, because the discipline is still an emerging one compared to other disciplines we often work alongside (UX design, engineering, or product management, for example). It's no wonder we sometimes feel that few people in our own organizations really know our true worth. Sometimes we're still figuring it out for ourselves.

But we're not *that* new. The value of content design isn't completely unknown, unproven, or unquantified. Let's be honest: content design has been around long enough, and has made enough of a difference to businesses, organizations, and users all over the world, that we should all feel we're standing on firm ground by now.

Do you feel like you're standing on firm ground?

You're not alone

The content people I talk to tell me they feel hampered by process and politics, by a dearth of respect, and by a chronic lack of investment and head count. They're often solo practitioners working in a sea of people who clearly want and need their help, yet don't consider them to be strategic partners. They say they're brought into projects too late to be of any but the most superficial assistance, and are rarely, if ever, given the chance to demonstrate clearly what they can do.

Does any of this sound familiar?

Here's what I'm guessing. I'm going to bet you're already really freaking good at your job. I bet you have incredible editorial, content-strategy, and content-design chops. And for the skills you still want or need to develop, you have the wherewithal to find the books, courses, and conferences that can help. (You can even start with the Resources section of this book.)

I'm also betting that you long for the chance to exercise some of those content chops even more—that what you really struggle with is the chance to do the work you know you can do, at the right stage of the game, with partners and stakeholders who know exactly the strategic value your presence brings.

You're tired of being pulled in at the eleventh hour to provide the "magic word" that will make a poorly planned product launch suddenly snap into sense, when the real problem is that no one clearly articulated the target audience for it eight or twelve months ago—when, as usual, you weren't in the room.

If that sounds like you, you know firsthand the pain of polishing content that has been built on a faulty foundation. It feels like you're always frosting a really terrible cake, but you don't know how to get your hands on the recipe book—how to change the way content works in your organization.

You might be thinking, *That's why we need to hire more writers and content designers for my team.* Or, *That's why we need to change our project management process, so I'll be involved in projects from the start.*

But I will firmly yet lovingly disagree. Because while these solutions might help in the short run, they won't really strike at the heart of the matter. If the teams you want to embed with don't know what content people can do, it won't do you much good to hire an army of writers. And, frankly, you're unlikely to get more people hired unless people at the higher levels of your organization have a real, bone-deep understanding of what it is people like you can do and how your work advances your company's real business needs.

People don't get a bone-deep understanding of something by hearing you say it for the hundredth time. They get it when you show them what the work looks like when it's done right, when you meet them where they are, and when you use the language, metaphors, and metrics that matter to them.

More than anything right now, what you need is some way to create the conditions in which you can do great content design. That's what I hope to provide in this book: a way for you to stretch your wings and really get a whack at the full suite of content work that I call *full-stack content design.*

Full-stack content design

Full-stack content design can only become a reality across your whole team when they've had a sort of content conversion experience—when something so radical has happened that they've changed their minds, their approach, their entire outlook on life. It's what some people might call a fundamental psychic change. And keep in mind you'll probably have to go through a shift in mindset yourself. This book is here to help you do all of that.

I know. That sounds like a lot for a relatively small book. But it does offer a path forward if you're stuck. It offers a way out of feeling like it's you against the world, like the deck is stacked against you, like content can't win. Because that mindset is probably getting you nowhere. And if this book gets you anywhere, it'll be somewhere better than that.

This book covers principles I worked out for myself long before I was even working in tech. Since then, I've worked with other content people in a variety of different settings, on different team sizes and types, helping them find their voice, express the voice of their company, and grow the impact a content practice can have on their organization's success.

Will this book apply to every content person, on every team, everywhere? Certainly not. It's likely to be most useful to folks working in-house on a fast-growing product, marketing, or services team. You might have to tweak it to your own purposes here and there. But regardless of your situation, it can work for you if you give it a try.

The change starts with you

Before you can change how other people see you, you're going to have to change how you see—and present—yourself. You know you're much more than just a proofreader and polisher of punctuation. You're a full-stack content designer, or you wouldn't have picked up this book.

You know that full-stack content design involves much more than just correcting grammatical errors or striking the right tone; after all, it does little good to correct Oxford commas if the ideas, format, structure, or delivery method aren't the right fit for the audience and their needs. That's why full-stack content design has to start with scoping out projects and deciding on goals; continue through research, testing, iteration, and change; and keep right on going through launch, publication, and continuous improvements.

But how do you get your hands on that kind of work?

What you need is to be working inside a full-stack content organization: one where every person on every team:

- sees the full content stack clearly,
- knows why it's important to the work *they* do,
- knows how to do some of it themselves to a baseline of proficiency, and
- knows when they're in trouble and need professional content help.

So the question really is this: How do you transform your organization into a full-stack content powerhouse?

It's a process, not an event

The process laid out in this book will help you change your organization from the inside out with love, empathy, and a deep concern for the things that matter most to the people you work with. Yes, you will find new ways to demonstrate how great content works and the value you offer. Better yet, you'll find new ways every day to drive real value in your company, and make a real difference in your coworkers' and customers' lives.

Because it's not about the silos that separate us in organizations. It's about how far we can go when we travel together.

Here's how it'll go:

- In Chapter 1, we'll explore how full-stack content design works. You'll get a clear picture of what it should look like, how you'll know if it's working, where it might need some help, and what you'll want to accomplish at each stage of the game.
- In Chapter 2, you'll learn how to spark a love of great content across your whole team, guide your colleagues to ask better content questions, and teach them how to use you as a strategic resource (instead of a human proofreading machine).
- In Chapter 3, we'll discuss how to design content workshops that speak meaningfully to your team's goals while opening hearts and minds to the real business impact of full-stack content work.

- In Chapter 4, you'll create a plan for prioritizing and championing great content at scale. You'll build on the strong culture you've created around content design, and you'll get more strategic about how you support others in their work.

The work does carry a risk of some intriguing side effects. Among other wonderful things, finding yourself within a full-stack content organization means you—and other content folk like you—will have the breathing room you need to be able to pick and choose where you can add the most value. It means you can step in and out of projects—or leave projects in others' capable hands—without needing to micromanage every little part of the content process yourself. You'll be focused on meaning, not minutia. And you'll have the power to be a real catalyst for change.

That change starts with you. It starts by changing your perception of the world you're operating in. It's not a world of us versus them, of people who love words and people who don't, of grammar fanatics and philistines. It's a world composed of people striving for an identical goal, curious about new ways to serve your customers as best you can. It's a world full of content champions, and content champions you just haven't activated yet.

This book is about how to ignite them—how to light them up from the inside with the power of content and create an organization that shines like a beacon of full-stack content design.

FULL-STACK
CONTENT DESIGN

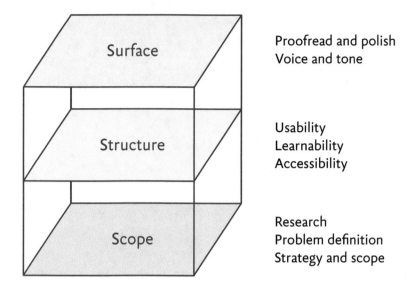

Surface — Proofread and polish / Voice and tone

Structure — Usability / Learnability / Accessibility

Scope — Research / Problem definition / Strategy and scope

FIG 1: A full-stack content design organization invests in and supports the people and practices that contribute to each layer of the stack.

MAYBE YOU'VE SEEN PEOPLE in other fields refer to themselves as "full-stack" practitioners. What they mean is they're able to contribute to the success of a project at every stage of the work, beginning to end, front to back.

Full-stack marketers, for instance, can gather data, analyze results, design experiments, run tests, create a complete marketing strategy, and do the tactical work of executing it. Full-stack engineers cover a similar breadth: backend, frontend, security, performance, testing, quality assurance. From soup to nuts, they can do it all.

Full-stack content designers play a strong role at every stage of the game, too: research and brainstorming, determining strategy and scope, sketching out flows, testing for usability and accessibility, proofreading and polishing the final result, measuring success and iterating based on the results. Soup to nuts. You can do it all.

To illustrate this range of contributions, I've reimagined the classic "Layers of UX" popularized by designer Jesse James

Garrett (http://bkaprt.com/ccd12/01-01/, PDF). Full-stack content design has three layers: Scope, Structure, and Surface (**FIG 1**). Each layer involves different types of content work: from level-setting and discovery, to creative output, to polishing and perfecting, rinse and repeat.

That's what full-stack content design is. It's not really about different stages of a chronological process, or different components of a final user experience. It's about the practices and people involved in creating digital content. Power up those people, invest in those practices, and you empower your process.

So what does this full-stack content design look like in practice? Let's take a closer look at each layer in turn.

SCOPE

The first layer is the place where everything starts (or should start, at least). It's the part of the process where you explore the problem space, discover what's possible, home in on your approach, and plan for everything that comes next in the project.

A content designer might be involved with a number of different activities in the Scope layer, usually across three areas of focus: research, problem definition, and strategy and scope.

Research

Content designers often work alongside researchers and analysts to write questions and scripts; conduct interviews; and parse, analyze, and present the results. And since content designers tend to be highly attuned to language and meaning, we often pick up on words, phrases, and cognitive pathways that others might miss. We hear it when users insist on a certain metaphor to describe what they're trying to do, and can craft interface copy that will match their mental model.

Working in partnership with researchers can be magical. The researchers I've worked with have often been delighted by the fresh perspectives a content person can bring to their work.

Finding one or two researchers who love working with you can be a great start to establishing a full-stack content practice.

Problem definition

Out of research comes the work of problem definition: working alongside product managers to articulate the problem the team is trying to solve. While the product manager often has a clear vision for this, a content designer can memorably capture it in the form of a written story, loosely illustrated storyboard, or user journey map.

Many teams start out trying to solve a different problem than the one that actually emerges from their research. That's not meant as a criticism—it's part of the process. You start in one place, do some research, and then refine your approach. That's why it's important to get very good at articulating the problem as you see it from the start, so you know just what it is you're refining as the research results start to roll in. Content designers help write the story of the problem, and then rewrite it over time.

There are many different ways a team might create a shared story to describe the core problem, such as a user journey map, a long-form narrative story, an illustrated storyboard, or a set of cartoons. They're all slightly different ways of pulling data points and details into one clear and compelling narrative arc for you and your team to rally around.

Clear and crisp problem definition is particularly important when you're working on a product with a broad and deep footprint, with teams that value rapid iteration and experimentation, or when coordinating work across multiple independent, autonomous teams on different pieces of the same cross-product user flow. Without clear problem definition, you might end up with different teams taking different stabs at the same problem; but with it, you retain small-team autonomy while keeping your goals and efforts aligned. Crafting a compelling story is also key for getting buy-in from leaders or stakeholders to move ahead with the project.

Strategy and scope

Part of the process of problem definition is deciding where to draw boundaries around your efforts. By corralling the project's purview and explicitly leaving aside what you won't be trying to solve, you can help your team avoid scope creep and stay focused.

Deciding on the scope of the project is in itself a strategic move. You're deciding that *this*, not *that*, is the challenge you're going to solve. A content designer can help a team make this decision clearly, and document it in a way that's easy for them to remember and share. A well-articulated scope, along with clear project definition, will help determine the strategic moves this project demands.

STRUCTURE

The Structure layer is where you start working on the organization, categorization, and hierarchy of ideas. It's where you begin designing your content to best meet users where they are without overwhelming, distracting, immobilizing, or annoying them.

Content designers will work with their team—often a mix of designers, engineers, information architects, and others—to present the solution to the problem with a focus on usability, learnability, and accessibility. These three areas often overlap, because they are mutually reinforcing, interwoven, and really inseparable at heart.

Usability

Usable content is designed with a careful eye toward how much cognitive load each step or stage carries, and creates consistency across the experience with the patterns the user has experienced elsewhere (in your product or in similar experiences in their life). Usable content makes sense to the user in the context of their own world.

This means your content uses metaphors, symbols, and language that already resonate with your audience. Usable content is inclusive content—you don't use words or elements that would only be comprehensible or welcoming to someone from a certain background, religion, gender, or class.

Learnability

Learnable content carefully considers which concepts might require explanation, clarification, or active practice to learn, and how to offer users the chance to learn them. The sequence, weighting, separation, combination, and organization of ideas, objects, actions, and assets are all factors in learnable content.

- It's important to consider what other experiences are already in the product (or are being worked on right now) and how those experiences might interact with or affect the experience at hand. As the resident content practitioner, you're likely to have a more holistic view of how different angles of the user experience come together across the whole product; the Structure layer is the best time to contribute that perspective.
- On a finer scale, you want to make sure the language and images you're planning to use match up with what's used elsewhere in the product. What metaphors or mental models are at play at other points in the experience? How might those metaphors extend to this project? How might they break down?
- It's often useful at this stage to assemble a simple inventory of the nouns (objects) and verbs (actions) most often used throughout the experience that are relevant to this project. Rather than undertake a full content audit, you might just gather a list of the objects and actions you're dealing with here. How do they fit (or not fit) the story you're trying to tell?

Accessibility

Your content won't be usable or learnable if it's not accessible, too. Designing your content for accessibility first will make it more inclusive, regardless of user circumstance, ability, or need.

Font size, color contrast, plain language, adaptability to screen readers, and much more all go into designing accessible content. Words need to be readable, in the sense that the user needs to be able to see and read the letters on the screen; and the text needs to be written at a reading level that optimizes comprehension. Text written at a sixth- or seventh-grade reading level is generally the most easily understood by all users, regardless of education level, industry, or background. Use the Resources section at the end of this book to learn more about who needs accessible content (spoiler alert: it's everyone) and how to write, structure, and design it.

You may come across people who resist your efforts to keep content at an accessible reading level. They may say you're "dumbing it down" or something equally offensive. You can tell them from me that the only thing that's "dumbed down" about accessible content is having an outdated, narrow, closed-minded idea of what "accessible" means.

Test early, test often

A common mistake at this stage is to get too invested in the words and images you're using to organize your design. Teams and individuals can easily latch on to words, images, naming conventions, and mental models that make more sense to them than to the user, which is why it's important to keep on testing and iterating with real users throughout the life of a project.

At this point, remember that your content is provisional, even placeholder content. Think of it as "low-fidelity" content you will refine over time. Some teams make it a practice to keep the images in early designs deliberately sketchy, unfinished, or at a low resolution, and to set the text in Comic Sans or something equally off-brand as a visual reminder that the content is provisional and subject to change.

SURFACE

The final Surface layer is where the content is refined and finalized. You already know which concepts and ideas are most important, and when and how they should be encountered and met. Content designers usually work alongside designers, marketers, support reps, and salespeople to make sure the experience they've designed aligns with the house style guide; fits into the larger user narrative arc; and is as easy as possible to understand, market, demo, sell, and support.

Proofread and polish

This is where UX writing and illustration come to the fore. You've been creating and testing low-fidelity content as part of the content design process so far. Now it's time to finalize your verbal, visual, and structural choices, and make them consistent with your house style in terms of spelling, grammar, punctuation, and form.

It's helpful at this stage to refer to some of your earlier work to inventory the words, images, and metaphors used across the rest of the product or experience to ensure your final product is consistent with them. If you've introduced any new terminology, concepts, or conventions, now's a good time to add them to your style guide and other internal glossaries or tools.

Voice and tone

It's also a good time to inspect your content for any voice or tone wrinkles, and to smooth them right out. Ensure that your words, images, and ideas are consistent with your brand voice, and that you're using the right tone for the situation at hand.

I like to think of *voice* as defining who you are—you're always you—while *tone* is how you behave in different situations. For example, I might define my own voice as friendly, helpful, quirky, and kind—but I'll present those aspects of my personality in different (and hopefully appropriate) ways, depending on whom I'm speaking to (my mother, my best friend, or the Queen of England) and the context of our conversation (a phone call, a dinner party, or getting a life peerage conferred).

You might notice that these late-stage activities on the Surface are the ones many people outside the content community tend to think we spend most (if not all) of our time on. But when you've been present and active at each stage of the game, the people you work with will have seen with their own eyes how important a role content plays from beginning to end.

START WHERE YOU ARE

You may feel you're stuck at the top of the stack, focused primarily on the Surface layer of content work. If you're on a product team, that means you're mostly spending your time on interface word choice and making minor adjustments to voice and tone. If you do marketing, tech writing, or internal communications, it might be more about copywriting, editing, and proofreading for house style. It's important work, and we tend to excel at it.

The first step in the full-stack mindset shift is accepting the reality of the top of the stack. While your natural impulse may be to bang on pots and pans and fight for a seat at the table farther down the stack, it's often more effective to start where you're already having an impact—right in the Surface layer.

It sounds counterintuitive, but hear me out. If you're stuck in an endless loop of proofreading and polish, start with the people you work with on that: designers, marketers, salespeople. They already know and trust you. You have a foundation of credit with them. These folks are likely to be your first converts—the content champions you'll enlist on your team.

Why not start by training these enchanting people to do some of this Surface work for themselves? Not all of it, naturally. But surely you can entrust some of the proofreading and polish to a group of enthusiastic trainees.

Moving a little Surface work off of your plate frees you up to go deeper into the stack. If you're currently buried in work at the top of the stack, and you *don't* enlist others' help, you'll never get that chance. And if nobody gets to see the deeper work you can do, they won't think to ask it of you in the future. It's a vicious cycle.

Hoarding your work also runs the risk of leaving talented people untapped. Literally every team I've ever worked with has had a handful of content enthusiasts lurking just under the surface, if you just give them a scratch. If you encourage and empower them even a little, these hidden content champions will surprise you with what they can do.

The goal isn't to never do Surface work again. It's to give yourself options. When you equip other people to do this work, too, you give yourself the gift of choice. You can choose to let them do it, or you can jump in and help out. There will always be lots of Surface work to be done, so you'll never stop the cycle if you don't find a way to let some of it go.

The downside is that you will no longer be the lone, magical wordsmith who works wonders behind closed doors. Sharing your skillset may erode some of the mystical glow around content design. And that's not a bad thing.

Because then you'll be free to rebrand yourself from magical wordsmith to problem definer, scope and strategy wrangler, accessibility advocate, and so much more. It's a simple question of bandwidth and branding.

STRIKE UP THE BAND

I'll say it again: you'll never get the chance to do the deeper stack work if you're swamped with Surface work that only *you* can get done. And if that's the only type of work people ever see you do, that's all that people will ever think you can do.

That's why the next step in this process is to help the people you work with recognize what good content looks like, understand the value of great content *to them in their roles*, and learn how to do at least some of that work for themselves.

And the way we do that is by getting everybody to sing the same song.

SING OUT LOUD

I ONCE WORKED WITH A GUY who was the king of earworms. Every once in a while, he'd try to see how long it would take him to get the whole office humming the same tune. He'd either walk down the hallway a few times, humming a few bars, or maybe he'd just scrawl a few potent lyrics on the whiteboard in a few conference rooms.

That's all it took, usually. And before lunchtime, we were all tapping our feet to the same jaunty beat.

We all have the power to drive change like that. The trick is to decide what song it is you want to put in people's heads, and then find a way to get it out into the world.

THE STYLE GUIDE TRAP

Content folk will often turn to their style guide to try to get people in their organization all singing the same tune. Usually when a company gets around to creating a house style guide, it's because they've discovered they have too many different people creating too much disparate content, and they want it to sound more like they're all singing the same song. Style guides are widely considered to be great tools for getting your team to start doing just that.

So why do we have such a hard time getting people to use them?

Maybe you've already noticed that the only people who actually read and use most style guides are the people who created them in the first place. Yeah, it's really just us. No matter how many times we urge other people to check the style guide, most of them don't.

And I truly don't blame them. The fact of the matter is that most people don't like or even understand style guides—what's in them, how to use them, why they even exist. Telling people to "use the style guide" is a bit like telling me I should keep a scientific calculator next to me at all times. Even if I were to follow such bizarre advice, I wouldn't know what to use it for, or even how. Honestly, its very presence would stress me out.

This is how most people feel when we remind them there are "writing rules" they need to follow. To most people, these rules are strange, oppressive, arbitrary, and unclear. The very fact that they exist at all stresses them out.

That's why, when we present ourselves as the Keepers of the Writing Rules, we tend not to get invited to things. We're a constant, visceral reminder that there are rules to this whole content situation, and that most people are probably breaking twenty of them at a time. Nobody likes having that person at their party, or meeting, or brainstorming session—that person is, frankly, a drag. Most people aren't at all sure what we'd have to offer besides sitting there and correcting everyone's grammar at will, which is a downer—and not even helpful most of the time.

So a major step in gaining control of our destiny has to be finding a different way of getting people to sing along with our song. And that means we need to learn to let go of our beloved style guides.

NOBODY CARES ABOUT YOUR STYLE GUIDE

Style guides are not teaching tools. They're sets of rules. People don't like to follow rules, because rules are not fun. But you know what's extremely fun? Writing great content. The trouble is, most people don't see the connection between the rules and the content.

Teaching other people to learn and apply the rules of writing is like insisting people learn to read musical notation instead of just helping them burst into song. You might know that it's key to making a strong composition, but they're pretty sure they'd rather skip right to singing a rock anthem at the top of their lungs.

They're not wrong. That's how people learn to love, support, and even make fantastic music themselves. You have to love it so much you can't help dancing along. Do you know how many great musicians never learned to read music? Let's start with Eddie Van Halen, Dave Grohl, Paul McCartney, Jimi Hendrix—shall I go on?

You need to find a creative way to get folks to sing along. The key is to find some lovable way to regularly get your song in front of them, all of the time. Whatever you can do routinely and do well—use that as a vehicle for your catchy style-guide tune. Some possibilities:

- **Posters.** Create a bunch of memorable posters for your office with visuals and text that show people what your voice and tone look like in action.
- **Wallpaper.** Create a series of delightful Zoom backgrounds for your distributed team. Replenish the supply often, so they never get stale.
- **Internal newsletters.** Never underestimate the power of an email newsletter, especially one that includes pictures of your adorable coworkers, their children, and their pets.
- **Blog posts.** Write about life at your company, profile some of your best customers, interview members of the leadership team.
- **Instagram posts.** Offer a peek into a day-in-the-life of a new employee, a user, the beloved barista who works down the street.
- **Curated playlists.** Use the power of music to quite literally get your team singing the same song.

If you look hard enough, you'll find a format that works for you, your goal, and your company, too. Do something different, something that doesn't exist today, for your team. If your company tends to wallow in words, use photography or illustrations to grab their attention and make them look up. If your company already has an internal newsletter or playlist, just start your own.

(And remember: you don't have to ask permission to start humming in the hallways. Often the unofficial, underground, guerrilla marketing methods are best.)

It all depends on where your strengths lie, and what your organization will respond to. Just do whatever you think will work best in your world. I used to joke that the right batch of temporary tattoos could do the job, and I stand by that. Content is content. Come on. You're good at this stuff.

And that's the key, really. It has to be good. It has to be something people *want* to tune in to. They need to enjoy—love—it, want to sing it out loud in their car. Remember, this is meant to be their content rock ballad. Make them want to turn it up to eleven.

RAISE YOUR VOICE

When you start creating this catchy content, stay away from telling people *about* the rules at all—at this stage of things, at least. *Don't even make this content about content.* Whatever vehicle you choose to get your message across, use it as a means to show good content in action, not to dissect *how* it was made. You're trying to build a karaoke machine, not instruct the masses in musical theory. Make it look easy. Make it look *fun*.

I like to use an internal newsletter as my karaoke machine. But that's just because (1) I love writing newsletters, and (2) I have the honor of writing one at my company. It's called the WIN, which stands for Weekly Internal Newsletter, which is just what it is. Among other things, it's meant to be a lovable earworm that promotes our fantastic culture—who we are and what we believe, honor, and support—which extends to our company voice and tone.

The WIN is simple and streamlined, lighthearted and fun. *Because our house style is to create content that's simple and streamlined, lighthearted and fun.* That's the song I want to get into everyone's head.

Maybe your house style isn't lighthearted and fun. Maybe your challenge instead is to get your organization to create clear, unbiased content without a glimmer of spark. That's okay, too. You can demonstrate how clear, unbiased content doesn't need to be boring (and, in fact, shouldn't be—content can't be clear if you've put your audience to sleep).

Maybe your company is already drowning in internal newsletters. That's okay, too. Create content that those newsletters will want to include. Interview some employees. Profile some customers. Find a way to tell a story people will want to hear, and do it in a way that shows your house style in action. I do love an internal newsletter, and I put it to you that even if you have loads of them already, it's quite possible yours will leave them all in the dust. So don't knock it till you try it, is all I suggest.

It doesn't even need to be that much of a lift. Here's how it works for my newsletter:

1. Every Wednesday, I send out a quick reminder that everyone is invited to submit to the WIN. This is usually just a fun illustration that matches the season, or something positive and unifying going on in the world, like reminding everyone that they love rescue puppies, or springtime.
2. Other people in the company will respond with a link to something they wrote that they want to promote—usually something that's just gone live on the company wiki. I don't know about your company, but we live and breathe on our internal wiki. (If it's not on the wiki, it didn't happen.) So if somebody wants to make sure the thing they wrote on the wiki has a fighting chance of getting seen by everyone at the company, they send it in to the WIN.
3. I add the link to the WIN—I've imposed a fairly arbitrary limit of just nine items, tops—with some zippy copy to promote it.

This last step is the key ingredient of the WIN, often forgotten when people start their own internal newsletters: I don't write any of the content that gets linked in the WIN. It's purely an act of curation on my part. This radically trims down the amount of time I have to spend on it, and makes it much more a snapshot of the company at that moment in time. It's not about me—it's about the people around me. All I do is write the copy that entices readers to click through to the submitted wiki post. That's it.

But that's everything. Because, honestly, most people *don't* click through. They just read my zippy copy. And that's okay, too, because that copy is written relentlessly in our house style, voice, and tone. It's brief, lighthearted, inclusive, optimistic, and fun. People read it, they get it, they internalize it over time.

And eventually, they realize that it has something they want.

WHAT A HERO WANTS

Remember: everybody at your company is a hero in their own story, too. And as we already know from crafting narratives, every hero has to want something.

What they want might not be to sound more like you (although they might say that when they email you after enjoying your catchy content for a few weeks or months). What they want is to reach that goal they have in their head. Hit their monthly sales target. Attract more great leads. Connect with customers more clearly. Win some executive buy-in. Writing in the voice and tone you've demonstrated is just a means to an end.

And what happens next, which absolutely will follow like night follows day, is that people very much want their content to sound more like that voice. They can't put their finger on it, but they know their content doesn't quite have that hook. And they want it to.

1. Does that sound too good to be true? I've seen it happen in all kinds of organizations, on all kinds of teams, in a wide variety of industries with different needs. I've seen it work for the dozens of people I've coached through the process.
2. We tend to forget—or at least grossly underestimate—that content created by someone who knows what they're doing will stand out from the crowd. When a talented writer puts strong content in front of people who need it, those people will take notice. And they will want to learn how to capture those skills for themselves.

HAVE FUN STORMING THE CASTLE

Instead of hammering at the rules, you built an attractive Trojan horse for your style, voice, and tone. Now you're quietly tiptoeing into everyone's inbox (or whatever) and getting them to sing along to something they actually enjoy, all while you slowly, stealthily get your brand voice and, yes, even style rules stuck in their head. As long as it's content they want to consume, they will start to internalize it, mimic it, and embrace it, *en masse*.

And that's exactly what you wanted to happen when you started this whole thing. It's all going according to plan.

WORKSHOPS THAT WORK

STOP ME IF YOU'VE HEARD THIS ONE: Somebody on the sales team wants you to look over the standard email they send to their best leads, to make it sound more human and friendly. Someone on the marketing team asks you for feedback on a landing page format that just isn't converting the way they think it should. Someone on the legal team wants to know how to make their dry and dusty terms of service sound less like legalese.

If you're a solo content person, or even part of a very small content team, you're probably quite used to these casual requests for editorial help. They always "should only take a minute," and, usually, they do. But those minutes pile up, don't they?

Now that you've been humming a catchy content tune all over the place, people are going to be asking you for help more than ever before. You might find these cries for help flattering, even fun to work on, but they may also be a source of additional stress on your workload. So why am I suggesting you generate even more?

Because you're going to start using these requests to grow your organization's content chops. From now on, when people ask you for tips, you're going to give them something even better than that.

You're going to suggest that you offer your best tips and tricks in the form of a *workshop for their whole team*.

I LIKE THE WAY YOU WORKSHOP

You might be surprised by how many people will think a workshop is a fantastic idea, so don't be shy about suggesting it. You're an expert they respected enough to ask for advice, and they'll be grateful for your time, energy, and support. They asked for your help because they think you're good at this stuff. And when you tell them to bring along their whole team, it means you're willing to share that knowledge with more people, which will make their jobs easier, too.

Running content workshops for teams that ask for your help will allow you to scale what you do like nothing else. But you're likely not already in the habit of running these kinds of workshops. You may be very well versed in the kind of workshop that tends to happen on design and UX teams, full of Post-it notes and ideation sprints and maybe the occasional improv game. I love improv games. But this isn't going to be that kind of workshop.

You're going to develop a very particular style of workshop—one designed to help teams tackle, for themselves, some vital component of your full-stack content practice.

No matter which layer of the content stack your hypothetical team needs help with, your workshop will follow the same five basic steps:

1. Do your research.
2. Diagnose the problem.
3. Find your five.
4. Terrible-ize it.
5. Teach your team.

The first four steps here are preparatory and will help you structure the format and content of the workshop itself, tailoring the message to what each team needs to hear most. The final stage, the workshop itself, is about an hour in length. Let's go through each step in turn.

DO YOUR RESEARCH

Start where any project starts: with basic research. In order to diagnose the problem this team needs help with, work with your contact person on the team—the one who originally asked you for help—to define:

1. the *container* for the content in question;
2. the *content* itself, also known as the message; and
3. the *goal* of the content, which you'll measure with an agreed-upon metric.

This part of the process is vital, so make sure to give yourself enough time to gather your notes and customize your workshop to the problem at hand. Your goal here is to deliver a workshop that opens this team's eyes to the full suite of content design as it applies to their jobs, so it's well worth the time it takes to fully prepare.

The container

Your first source document will be the original piece of content your contact brought to your attention. Ask yourself: What's the nature of the content they want help with? For example:

- A product team wants to write error messages that will reduce support calls.
- A sales team wants to create an email that will help them book demos.
- A marketing team wants to build a higher-converting landing page.

Error messages, emails, landing pages—these are all *containers* for the content you'll be working on. They're the delivery vehicles for the team's messaging.

It's possible that the container they're using isn't the right one for the message and goal, and that's something you might encourage the team to question during the workshop. It's a major teachable moment when you can get a team to see that in order to achieve the goal they have for this content, they might need to go deeper than adjusting the subject line or tone. But for now, the important thing is to help them see that there's a distinction between the content and the container, and that they can make choices about each.

The content

Next, identify the meaning of the *content* within that container. What's the message they're trying to get across? For example:

- The error message should tell the user what's wrong and what they can do next.
- The sales email should tell the user there's a solution to their problem.
- The landing page should convince the user that attending a webinar will answer their questions.

You'll often find that a piece of content is primarily concerned with getting the user to understand something new, or in a new way. It should also offer the user an action they can take as result, which is tied to the content's goal.

The goal

Now that you know what the content is and what it's trying to communicate, you can identify its *goal*—the action taken by the user—and how the team measures the success of that goal. For example:

- The product team wants users to return to the login screen and try logging in again, measured by the number of users who successfully log in after getting this error.
- The sales team wants their email recipients to book a live demo, measured by the number of demos booked every month through that email's link.
- The marketing team wants people to reserve a spot in their webinar, measured by the number of people who register using that landing page's link.

Defining the metric is a key part of planning the content workshop, since it allows you to clearly and explicitly tie what you teach them to the metrics that govern the world they live in. You've got to gear the whole thing around the metrics that matter to them.

Make sure the metric is clearly measurable and has real business value to the team. It should be a metric that keeps them up at night, one that makes a regular appearance on their monthly meeting slides or performance reviews.

Ask them for the actual baseline number for this metric that they're hitting right now. Then ask them to tell you what a good outcome would be. What *should* that number look like? That's your shared goal. You are now all on the same team, clearly, explicitly, trying to achieve the same ends.

DIAGNOSE THE PROBLEM

Once you've compiled all this research—what type of container you're dealing with, what the content is supposed to make the reader think or do, and how to know if it's working—verify your conclusions with your team contact. It's important that you go into this workshop speaking the team's language—that the way *you* think about the container, content, and goal is perfectly aligned with how *they* think about them.

Ask your contact to gather different examples of the same type of content from other folks on the team. You don't need a million of them—about five or six will do nicely. You just want to get a representative sample of what they're using today.

Once you have these in hand, read through them slowly. Resist the urge to edit them as you go along. That urge will be strong. All you're really doing at this point is trying to decide where the team needs the most help: at the Surface layer, the Structure layer, or the Scope layer.

Surface challenges

Content that has challenges primarily at the Surface layer will be rife with errors of style, voice, and tone—but that's all that's really wrong with it. Ask yourself: If you fixed all of the grammatical errors, bad sentence formation, misjudgments of your brand voice, or tone misalignments, would it be fine? Or are there deeper, more serious problems lurking beneath? Can this content be saved purely by giving more attention to the process of proofreading and polishing? Or does the problem extend beyond that, into the content structure itself?

Structure challenges

Structure problems are a bit harder to diagnose, especially if there are also a lot of Surface issues to distract your eye. Ignore those for now, and look closely at the content's information order, hierarchy, usability, and accessibility. Are the sentences, paragraphs, menu options, or flow in the right order, or do they need a complete overhaul? Is the meaning clear? If you corrected all the Surface problems, would it still be a mess?

There is some potential overlap here with Surface issues, of course, especially when it comes to diagnosing problems related to usability, learnability, and accessibility. Many companies consider it an issue of house style to choose shorter words, avoid jargon, and use plain language—all core usability considerations. But questions of usability tend to raise deeper issues than just changing one word out for another. Adjusting the reading level of a whole document usually requires a more wholesale approach, often rethinking the structure and scope of the document. So while I agree in principle that content usability can and should be addressed in a style guide, I find that solutions to these issues typically require a much deeper dive than pure Surface problems do.

Scope challenges

Content with problems at the Scope layer tends to be unclear on what that user's next step might be, or—more often—offers too many possible next steps to pursue. *Either call your senator or write them or donate or email us for more details.* That's a serious muddle. It's content that is trying to do too much at once.

I'd argue that "one" is the right number for suggested next steps (also known as the *call to action*, or CTA) in any given piece of content. (Maybe two, if you count the option of "No, thanks.") Content should convince you to book a demo now—or don't. Update your account info now—or don't. Call your senator—or assume somebody else will do it for you. Those are your options. Do or do not. There is no try.

If you suspect you're dealing with problems at the Scope layer, revisit your notes about the content's goal. Is the action getting diluted by a lot of *ifs, ands,* or *buts?* If so, go back to your contact person and ask them to clarify the content's goal. What's the *one* action they want the reader to take?

Watch out if the answer is something like "be aware." We generally write content to convince users to *do* something. Sometimes that involves an intermediary step of learning or gaining awareness. But the next step is almost always, "So now do this thing." If that isn't clear in the content, you know to focus on Scope discussions in your workshop.

Once you've diagnosed the problem and determined whether the greatest need is to address the Surface, Structure, or Scope of the content, it's time to move on to the next step.

FINDING YOUR FIVE

Say you've gotten a nice, representative handful of emails from a sales team—samples of the emails they send to prospects who might want to book a demo or contact a sales rep. They don't know what, exactly, is wrong with the emails, but they know they're not working as well as they should. And since they've tried everything else—sending them more often, less often, earlier and later in the day or on different days of the week, and so on—they reckon it has to do with the content itself.

At first glance, you can spot Surface problems. They have a bunch of minor bad habits that, taken together, are keeping their readers from getting on board with the whole demo idea. The order, flow, and amount of information looks fine, and they're not trying to do too much or too little with this one piece of content, either. There's a single, clearly stated CTA at the end. Okay. This baby needs some proofreading and polishing help.

You take a closer look still. Like a lot of people these days, these content creators tend to rely on commas and run-on sentences to establish a breezy, conversational tone. For instance, one of the sample emails starts out:

Hey [name]!
*Thanks so much for visiting our site the other day, hope you
found what you needed!*

You jot down something about overusing exclamation marks
and comma splices, and sip your tea for a second or two while
you ponder whether "Hey" or "Hi" would be the most appropriate greeting in an email like this. You double-check your source
material and, sure enough, this team is focused on reaching
people in the US, mostly in entry-level roles, in a fairly casual
industry, where a lighthearted voice is desired. So kicking
things off with a low-key, casual "Hey" is probably just the
ticket. So that's okay.

You notice the content creators have a tendency to say "our
software" and "our site" more than they talk about "your needs"
and "your team,' so you'll want to talk to them about who pro-
nouns say is really the hero around here.

They might lean a bit too hard on needlessly longer words
when a shorter word will do, like saying "utilize" instead of
"use," or "leverage" instead of *literally any other word at all*. Also,
there's an "incentivize" in there. Ew. Okay, you'll make sure to
talk about plain language and short words.

You keep going, working your way through your documents
until you've found five things you want this team to work on.
Five things—that's all.

Keep it simple

You're not trying to compile a list of every mistake they
make—you're looking for the top five issues that, if addressed
in a uniform way, would significantly raise the effectiveness
of their work.

Any more than five things and you run a real risk of overwhelming them. The message you want them to walk away
with isn't, "Wow, content is super complex and hard," or "Gosh,
I've been doing content so incredibly wrong." It's, "I can do this!
I just need to do these five simple things." The confidence you
give them in this workshop is just as important as the guidance
you impart.

You know that there's a lot more to this than just five simple rules. But you also know that if they just did these five things differently, every single time, they'd see a difference in the content and in how well it does the job they're asking it to do.

Along with your five simple rules, you'll also show them the tools and resources available to help them, most of which, I promise you, they don't yet know exist. Or they might have heard of them (rumors of a style guide, whispers of voice-and-tone guidelines carried on the wind), but they don't really have any sense of why they might want to access them. Now they'll understand what those resources can do in the context of their own work.

Try to keep the workshop focused on just one content layer: Surface, Structure, or Scope. There's usually plenty to keep you occupied within just that one realm, and a tightly focused workshop will yield far better results.

By the end of this workshop, they'll be adept at navigating a layer of the stack as it applies to their content (which matters a great deal to them), and they'll see how investing in that layer will help them reach their team goals.

TERRIBLE-IZE IT

Now comes the best part: creating a composite version of the content that is absolutely *the worst*.

Take your team's sample content and wildly exaggerate the worst traits you've identified. If they're abusers of exclamation marks, put these everywhere. Comma splice fanatics? Leave no sentence unspliced. Push the needle on whatever five things you've decided to focus on and turn the awfulness all the way up to eleven. Make it really, *really* smelly and bad.

This accomplishes two important things: First, it makes the sample content you're going to ask them to work on at the end of the workshop so unrecognizable that no one on the team will feel bad or singled out. It'll be recognizable as the kind of content they need help with, but comfortably terrible enough that they know they're at least better than *that*.

Second, editing content that has been expertly terrible-ized is a surprisingly effective way of getting people to remember the rules you're teaching them. Subtlety isn't memorable; over-the-top, laugh-out-loud, cringeworthy content is.

And third (I know I said two things but I'm a writer, not a mathematician): terrible-izing content is fun. It's fun for you to do before the workshop—you will giggle a lot—and it's fun for the team when you give it to them to fix.

Remember the sage words of one of my dearest friends, who likes to remind me that "the second most powerful human urge is editing other people's writing."

The first most powerful urge, of course, is overusing excla-mation marks. You can look it up.

TEACH YOUR TEAM

These workshops should never be more than an hour in length (again, you don't want to overwhelm people). The bulk of the time will be spent exploring the nature of the problem this team needs to solve, with about fifteen minutes at the end to work on the terrible-ized content.

Kick things off with an introduction to the layers of content design—Scope, Structure, and Surface—using something like the diagram found in this book. Give participants an overview of the work required to create quality content at each layer.

I find it helpful to ask them for a parallel in their own line of work. For instance, sales people often spend hours on research and planning before they get on a call, customizing their strat-egy and script to each potential customer—this can be a form of full-stack content design, too. Make them see that they're already content designers themselves, and that you're here to help them develop that muscle to hit their goals.

Spend the majority of your time going over the five princi-ples you identified as being most relevant to this team. Don't go out of your way to make it clear that this is based on the work they provided you at the start. The more accidental it appears, the more likely it is they will see you as a trove of relevant, use-ful information that will help them move the metrics that matter most to their team. Walk them through any documentation, resources, playbooks, or guidelines that you have in your content arsenal, and point out areas of potential interest to them.

For instance, if a team needs help with basic style and tone, I'll spend a lot of time on those areas (and less time on, say, usability recommendations). Did they know we have guidance on how to use exclamation marks? Turns out, we do! They will write down this fact. It will probably be news to them. And they will be delighted to hear it. Remember, most people are swimming around in murky, eel-infested waters when it comes to writing content; they are generally grateful if you can throw them a rope and lead them safely to shore.

If you don't have playbooks and guidelines for each case you encounter, that's okay. Designing these workshops can serve as your own discovery research, informing you about the needs of your users (the internal teams at your company) and the resources that will help them do their jobs. If your first few workshops seem to center on questions of voice and tone, that's a great excuse to spend some time either creating or refining the guidance you have.

As time goes on, you'll probably find that the workshops start naturally going deeper down the layers. You don't need to have playbooks and libraries of guidance on hand when you start doing this work. The work will inform what you need to create. All you need to do is stay one chapter—sometimes even one page—ahead of the people you're working with and trying to help.

BE THE GUIDE, NOT THE GURU

Before long, you'll be regularly running these workshops—introducing teams to the idea of full-stack content design, showing off the finer points of whatever documentation will help them, and concentrating on five basic principles that can change the way they work.

In return, your colleagues will start to see the pursuit of quality content as the treasure they seek. And they'll know that the resources you're offering them are the map for that quest.

You might be uncomfortable with this, at first, if you're very secure in your role as the Keeper of the Words in your organization. But the more you shift how you see yourself—and how you're willing to be seen—the more you'll be able to empower the people around you. You're a fellow traveler who has been down these roads before, and you're ready to help your teammates successfully find their way through the content stack, too.

CONTENT AT SCALE

ONE OF THE MOST STARTLING effects of this process occurs when it all starts to work. One day you will wake up to an embarrassment of riches. You'll have multiple requests for content help, and it will *all* be of the kind you've been wanting to do. High-level, early-stage, strategic work. Full-on structural overhauling and rebuilding of an existing system or service. Gloriously engaging voice-and-tone work for a flow that serves a key user need.

Once you show people what you can do—and clearly demonstrate to them how it impacts the success metrics they care most about—the floodgates will open, and you'll suddenly have way too much work.

Wait. What? Wasn't this book supposed to help you *scale* what you do? Become more efficient, more selective, and *not* spread so thin?

Yes, and it absolutely will do all of that. But once you reach this inflection point—where you've officially teetered over from not-enough-of-the-right-kind of work to wanting to hide on a small island somewhere with an unlisted number—you've got a totally different problem on your hot little hands.

It's at this point that I would urge you *not* to start arguing for headcount. I know, I know, I'm such a buzzkill. But this is probably the most delicate stage of the proceedings, and it's so important that you don't rush. You're the one who promised you could do all this great work—so, at least for a while, you're the one who has to deliver the goods.

Now you need to get serious about how you'll prioritize the work.

PICKING YOUR PRIORITIZATION PLAN

The great news is there's no lack of handily acronymed prioritization protocols out there. You can take your pick. It's possible your team already uses something to prioritize their projects, but you might find it wasn't designed with full-stack content work in mind.

Don't be shy about developing your own approach to prioritizing your work. Remember, you're in charge of your own story. You get to decide if the narrative is "I have too much work" or "I have so many valid requests for work that I triage and support them in several different, equally effective and appropriate ways." I know which story I'd rather be in. But, hey, you do you.

For my money, any prioritization system that gives you a clean, numerical score is a workable plan. You may be quantifying highly subjective information, but you're not just conjuring numbers out of thin air; ideally, you're developing them in consultation with the stakeholders who want your help with something.

Start with a full and frank exchange of views with your stakeholders. How do they prioritize their own work today? If they already use a clear prioritization plan, see if you can extend it to the work you do. What considerations do they weigh when prioritizing projects? It might be a combination of things like how many users this project will impact, to what extent, how much effort and time it will take, and what the payoff will be. Maybe they already weigh considerations like these, and you can work together to figure out where this project falls on each sliding scale.

Maybe they go more on gut feel, or whichever project has the loudest voice arguing for it. Hey, it happens. That might be a great opportunity to gently suggest factoring in more quantifiable aspects, too. The important thing is that you work alongside your partnering teams to come to an agreed-on and shared prioritization plan. You're setting expectations in terms of value, impact, and timeline, so it's worth taking the time to get it right—and in writing.

It has to be a collaborative process. Disappearing into a dark room somewhere and emerging hours later with a carefully ordered list of how you'll prioritize your work will get you nowhere fast. Working through the concerns, needs, goals, and fixations of your partnering teams, on the other hand, will keep your work—and its impact on their success—top of mind.

Remember what they used to say in math class: *show your work*. Getting to the right answer is no victory at all if we don't get there together.

When priorities attack

When you need to choose between a variety of projects that are all clamoring for your attention and you simply don't have the bandwidth to do them all, it's time to take a different approach. Maybe for a while you've been able to use your prioritization simply as a method of ordering when you'll do each project and how much time you'll commit to each one. But at some point, you'll realize you can't do it all. That's when it's time to call in the cavalry and outsource some of your work to other people and tools.

Surface work can sometimes be handled by someone on the team who has attended your Surface workshop (see how that works?) or by some form of automation to smooth out the rough edges. If nobody on the team has taken your Surface workshop, you might book one for them now.

At HubSpot, we created an internal editor tool that applies the rules of our style guide and offers suggestions and corrections when it finds a mistake. Content creators simply paste their content into the tool, and the tool highlights the errors, offers hints and suggestions for revision, and links to the relevant part of the style guide for more detail.

This tool was based on an earlier, open-sourced version of something similar that's still available today, so building your own version might not be as much of a pipe dream as you think. It's fully worth the time required to create and maintain it, since it takes the most repetitive Surface corrections (spelling, punctuation, clichés, jargon, and so on) off your plate. Check out the Resources section for more ideas about building your own editor bot.

Surface work can also, in a pinch, be handled by a free tool like Grammarly or Hemingway. Are free tools ideal? Will they strictly follow your own style guide? Probably not. But asking people to use available tools before coming to you can free up an enormous amount of your time. Remember, since your time is best spent on the deeper layers of the stack, your job is to:

1. teach and empower other people in your organization to do more Surface work themselves, and
2. establish which tools they can use to check their Surface work without your help.

It takes a little time and effort to get the machinery in motion, but you'll soon be able to teach, delegate, and automate your way out of the morass of Surface work.

The hardest part of this process is actually letting the Surface work go. It is hard, in the moment, to say no to someone who asks you to give something a "quick look." But acquiescing not only keeps other people from learning and applying these skills and becoming more self-sufficient; it also reinforces in their minds that this is the only kind of work you do. Let it go.

Finding support

At some point, even the number of high-priority projects you're able to handle at the speed they need to be completed will become too much. Everyone will agree that your bandwidth has reached its limits. And *this* is where the conversation about headcount usually starts.

When the teams you're working with have had a direct hand in helping you build out your roadmap, yet there are still plenty of high-complexity, high-risk problems that need content support, that's usually when the teams themselves start advocating for headcount. The stakes are simply too high not to invest resources now. They'll move heaven and earth—and often, their very own headcount allocation—to get the content support they now know they need.

It's also possible you'll just have to work with what you have. Not all organizations will be able to hire new dedicated content people, no matter how much they'd like to. This may be due to economic hardship, the growth stage of your company, or a million other things that have nothing to do with how respected or valued you and your abilities are.

Whoever your organization is equipped to empower with content responsibilities can be your new team of content designers. Maybe it will be a cross-functional group that wants to run point for content needs on their team. Maybe it will be a blend that will evolve over time. The point is not to get too tied to a particular mechanism, job title, or organizational structure for improving the quality of content work overall. It's almost always more effective to take a pragmatic approach and work with what you've got.

Of course, by now, you're doing a lot to add more arrows to this particular quiver. By getting good content in front of people as often as you can, by running workshops that teach them how to help themselves as much as they can, you're building your organization's content capabilities by leaps and bounds. Not by fighting for headcount or by adding complexities to anyone's process—just by leading the way, showing your work, trusting the capabilities of others, and cultivating content champions wherever you can.

Even if you're the only content person in your organization, you can have an outsized impact by working with others who can share the load, and by focusing your efforts more and more on the deeper layers of the full content stack.

SUPPORTING A CONTENT PRACTICE

Regardless of job title, people all over your organization now care deeply about content because they've seen how it affects the work they do. How can you keep cultivating this newfound culture of content? How can you keep your new army of content folks interested, engaged, and sharp?

Whether you hire people from outside or just work with the people already on hand, you'll need the same systems to support them and keep them in tune. There are a number of ways to support the practice of content at your organization, no matter which or how many people are involved in the pursuit.

Content critiques

Give colleagues a chance to teach and learn from one another by setting up a regular time for them to share their in-progress content work, ask for feedback, and improve their skills in the context of a lovingly rendered content critique.

Peer-to-peer learning doesn't just improve the content under scrutiny; it also helps content creators think more deeply about their writing. Perspectives from other writers on other teams operating in other business contexts can lead to new approaches and results. And inviting people from all over the company to attend can widen the circle of colleagues who understand the scope of full-stack content design.

Most people will get heartburn at first when you suggest they put their rough drafts in front of their peers for feedback, so it's helpful to set some ground rules that will put people at ease. A good content critique follows much the same format as a good design review, so consider running yours along the same lines. Look in the Resources section for more help with running good critiques.

Content book club

Books clubs are perennially popular ways to get people engaged in a subject, talking about issues, and staying up to date with the latest thinking in the field. I've seen people get scared off by the level of commitment involved in a traditional book club, however, so you might consider framing this as more of a reading club that shares and discusses briefs, articles, talks, blog posts, or books.

But don't just set up a Slack channel to share links; without accountability of some sort, few will take the time to read most of what's shared, so make sure you plan regular opportunities to discuss as a group. You can set up recurring reminders to help people remember what you'll be discussing next, and who will be responsible for leading the conversation. It's often a good idea to rotate responsibility for facilitating the discussion so no one person is always on—or off—the hook every time.

Content networking

Set up time to chat with content people at other companies you admire. This can be a mutual "ask me anything" session where you talk about things you've learned or are still struggling with. How do they approach project prioritization? How do they do content work across the full stack? What has worked for them as they've scaled and grown their content practice over time? What hasn't worked out so well?

Not sure where to find such lovely people to chat with? You can start with the people you talk about in your book club. Authors, podcast hosts and their guests, people doing interesting work mentioned in books and articles, conference speakers you've seen in person or on YouTube, people you've connected with (or would like to connect with) on LinkedIn—the list goes on. If you don't feel you have the network required for this sort of thing, that's kind of the point. Forcing yourself to reach out to people in the industry you'd like to learn from is how they all started, too.

Thirty-day writing sprints

For the people who ask you how to get better at writing, the answer is: practice. Challenge these folks to a thirty-day sprint of writing for fifteen minutes every day, with the goal of getting to what the writer Anne Lamott calls a "shitty first draft."

You can set up an informal sprint group and support each other with daily prompts. This will keep folks from trying to get too fancy (developing fully fleshed-out blog posts, or writing the Great American Novel, for instance) when the goal is to get comfortable with the practice of dumping words out of your brain. Tell them they can worry about the editing and shaping of it later.

The stripped-down version of this writing sprint practice is really:

1. write like crap
2. every day
3. about not much at all

And it actually works. In fact, it's the *only* way to get better at writing, as we writers know. If you can recruit content creators when they're on fire with enthusiasm for writing and content—and many will be after attending one of your fabulous workshops—they'll have a real shot at developing their writing skills in this way. Even if they only stick to it for a couple of weeks, they'll learn very quickly how to keep typing through thick and thin.

THE BIG PICTURE

Imagine no longer seeing your job as a series of battles to be fought, no more us against them, no more peering over your reading glasses at the philistines who just don't get how you feel about exclamation marks, and never will. A healthy, full-stack content ecosystem creates a culture in which not just content professionals, but *everyone* who touches content, can truly grow, expand their impact, and thrive.

Once you commit to establishing a full-stack content practice in your organization, once you shift your focus to educating and empowering all the non-writers in your company to step into their power as content superheroes, that's when it happens. That's when the mindset shift starts to take hold. And that's when people start asking you to contribute in the very ways you've been hoping to.

CONCLUSION

SO MUCH OF THIS BOOK has been about the subtle art of letting go. And there's a good reason for that.

We agreed at the start of this conversation that we, as content people, need to get over ourselves and our need to *own all the words*. It's just not helping, that attitude. It doesn't get us a seat at the table. It doesn't demonstrate our value. It doesn't really achieve much of anything except an inner sense of smugness and victimhood.

So let's just stop. Let's replace that attitude with one that conveys our enthusiasm, empowers our colleagues, and lightens our loads.

The point isn't to teach and train and automate our way out of a job. The point is to encourage absolutely everybody in our organizations to own some part of the job of content design, so they all:

1. have a clearer idea of what the full stack of content design truly entails and can do for their goals,
2. know where and how they can contribute to great content themselves, and
3. recognize when it's time to call in a specialist—a content pro like you and the folks on your (soon-to-be-growing) team.

Steps one and two will help you clear the decks so you can pick and choose where you spend your quality time. Step three will make it clear if and when you need to add strength to your team.

None of this has a dang thing to do with where we all stand on the use of an Oxford comma, I'm afraid. But it does have to do with giving you your life and sanity back. It will also give you the chance to see light bulbs come on in the minds of your colleagues, illuminating your shared problem spaces with crisp, clear, compelling content that *everyone* has had a hand in creating.

Once you've achieved all that wonderfulness, it's time to kick back and enjoy the fruits of success. Wait, no, that's not right either. Because this is when the real work truly begins.

Nobody is better situated to keep a beady eye on what it is we're persuading others to believe—about ourselves, our products, and the way the world works—than content folks are. Content can convince people the world is a terrifying place that's relentlessly spiraling downward. Or it can say there's some good in this world, Frodo, and it's worth fighting for.

Everything you do—as a professional, as a team leader, as an encourager, as an aspiring strategic seat holder—tells the world who you are and what you stand for. Seeking out and supporting the hidden writer in everyone sends a message that we're all in this together. That together we win.

It's a pretty big deal to finally get that seat at the table you've been clamoring for. It's an even bigger deal when you manage to build your own table and invite everyone to join you in creating something new. Now that you have a growing and carefully cultivated content practice in your organization, what are you going to do with it?

ACKNOWLEDGMENTS

THANKS TO EVERYONE WHO told me that writing this book was a terrific idea, starting with Kristina Halvorson, who said it first. Thanks also to Dan Tyre, Richard Waystack, Hannah Fleishman, Danielle Kowalski, Scott Kubie, and Jami Oetting, who either encouraged me at the outset or egged me on every step of the way. Sarah Winters and Aaron Burgess both reviewed an early manuscript of this book and gave me valuable feedback and love, for which I am grateful beyond words. Ann Handley took me out for dinner and reassured me that I wasn't alone in my lifelong love for newsletters and what they can do.

Thanks to Christopher O'Donnell, Josh Porter, Tim Merrill, and Libby Maurer, who supported and sponsored the growth of content design at HubSpot before many product people even knew what it was. Thanks to Brian Halligan, who didn't blink when I cornered him in a hallway in 2010 and told him HubSpot needed an internal newsletter, said that sounded fantastic, and let me take it from there. Thanks to everyone at HubSpot who has loved, read, and submitted to the WIN. Writing this newsletter and serving as an amplifier for the unique personality and verve of this remarkable company has always been the best part of my job. Thank you for letting me hold up a mirror to you every week and remind you what excellent people you are.

RESOURCES

There are a handful of books and links I recommend to people whenever they ask me where to get started with content design. This isn't by any means an exhaustive list, but it's a good place to begin.

- Sarah Winters wrote the book *Content Design* (under the name Sarah Richards) and gave us all a focus and framework for what content design was and should be. Her emphasis on first doing content discovery and research, then centering the design on what the user actually needs (and not what the designer or organization wishes to say) was revolutionary when it came out and continues to be a definitive guide. This book also contains some very helpful recommendations for how to run effective content critiques, do pair writing, conduct user research, and develop several other practical skills.
- See also her team's *Readability Guidelines,* which will help anyone who wants to make their style guide less focused on old-fashioned and frequently irrelevant rules of grammar and punctuation and more focused on how to create truly useful, accessible, inclusive content (http://bkaprt.com/ccd12/05-01/). Better yet, it's all based on evidence and research, rather than personal preference for this rule or that.
- We've been treated to a wave of sterling books recently on the nuts and bolts of UX writing. One that stands out is *Writing Is Designing: Words and the User Experience* by Andy Welfle and Michael Metts, both for its thoroughness and use of real-life examples, and for how it incorporates the voices of real people doing this work in a variety of industries and fields. Read this book to learn more about how to do great UX writing, and to get introduced to some of the smartest, kindest people working on it today.

- Rachel McConnell's book *Why You Need a Content Team and How to Build One* is a terrific resource for content people on teams of all sizes and stages of growth, from the solo practitioner to a large, globally integrated team. She helps you diagnose which stage you're in and what you might need to advance to the next level. It's an invaluable guide, especially if you're building a content team for the first time.
- Ann Handley's book *Everybody Writes: Your Go-To Guide to Creating Ridiculously Good Content* is what I give people who tell me they want to get better at writing but don't know where to start. It's empowering, practical, and down-to-earth. Ann's newsletter for writers, *Total Annarchy*, is a fortnightly infusion of insights, ideas, encouragement, and fun. Shenanigans, as Ann would say. It's one newsletter you will read, learn from, and laugh at, every time (http://bkaprt.com/ccd12/05-02/).
- Donna Lichaw's book *The User's Journey: Storymapping Products That People Love* will not just remind you how much you love the movie *Back to the Future*; it will also give you a clear, actionable model for how to apply the principles of storytelling to create truly user-centered experiences. A lot of people like to *say* the user is the hero, but then create content that's clearly centered on what the company wants the user to do. This book will snap you out of that trap. It's also a great book to give to people you work with, so you have a shared language and vision for what you're trying to do.
- Shopify built Rory, an editor bot that applies the rules of their style guide to their help documentation (http://bkaprt.com/ccd12/05-03/). It was adapted from an earlier, open-source editor tool called Alex (http://bkaprt.com/ccd12/05-04/). The source code for both Rory and Alex is available for anyone to use and adapt (although even open-source tools have license requirements, so make sure you comply with those). Alex comes complete with standard rulesets (for inclusive language, clichés, jargon, and more) that will likely apply to your style guide. Add a few rulesets specific to your house style, set it up on your server, and you're good to go.

- The Content + UX Slack group is a must for anyone interested in chatting about content design, learning more about UX writing, or meeting helpful, smart people who do great things with words. Ask questions, find a job, explore new topics, and make new friends from all over the world (http://bkaprt.com/ccd12/05-05/).

Content design is increasingly becoming a very large and boisterous party, one to which I'm delighted to report that newcomers and fresh perspectives are most heartily welcome. You'll find an open door to the party through any of these resources, but then you will quickly find yourself drawn into some fascinating side conversations and brilliant new friends to go deeper with. Please join us, and then tell us what you've learned.

REFERENCES

Shortened URLs are numbered sequentially; the related long URLs are listed below for reference.

Chapter 1

01-01   http://www.jjg.net/elements/pdf/elements.pdf

Resources

05-01   https://readabilityguidelines.co.uk
05-02   https://annhandley.com/newsletter/
05-03   https://ux.shopify.com/rorybot-automated-content-style-check-ing-4d42946ae318
05-04   http://alexjs.com
05-05   https://contentandux.org

INDEX

ABOUT A BOOK APART

We cover the emerging and essential topics in web design and development with style, clarity, and above all, brevity—because working designer-developers can't afford to waste time.

COLOPHON

The text is set in FF Yoga and its companion, FF Yoga Sans, both by Xavier Dupré. Headlines and cover are set in Titling Gothic by David Berlow.

ABOUT THE AUTHOR

Beth Dunn is a content and communications leader, speaker, author, and coach. She pioneered the content design practice at HubSpot, then developed and led the global HubSpot content design team. Her workshops, classes, exercises, and guides have helped scores of leaders, practitioners, and teams design better content, confidently and at scale. Beth Dunn lives on Cape Cod in her tiny hometown with a charming husband and some quality cats.

L - #0230 - 040521 - C62 - 216/140/3 - PB - DID3079784

Lacey's Last Chance

A Play Two Ways
One Act
Ten Minute

by Gabriel Davis

Lacey's Last Chance is a dark little comedy originally written as a short one act which, given the interest in plays of ten minutes or less, was subsequently trimmed to fit. What follows are both the long and the short form.

Lacey's Last Chance

A Play in One Act

by Gabriel Davis

gabriel@alumni.cmu.edu
www.gabrielbdavis.com/

CHARACTERS

Lacey
A woman in her mid twenties

Trent
A man in his mid twenties

SETTING
An empty stage
which becomes a Quickie Mart

(The actors shift between audience address and scene work throughout. *When they are speaking directly to each other it is denoted by italics*)

(LACEY enters a bare stage, and addresses the audience)

LACEY

My father was a wonderful man who waited on me hand and foot when I was a child. Mother used to jokingly call him "the slave." When I grew up, I expected to find a husband as loving and selfless as my father. Instead I found Frank.
(beat)
I would always give Frank thirty minute back rubs, which he always asked for. He'd never give me back rubs unless I begged, and then only for thirty seconds. One time, I broke both my arms and they were put in casts. Despite this I continued with Frank's back rubs. The doctor warned me that if I continued using the muscles in my arms that way, I would permanently damage them and have unbearable shooting pains for the rest of my life. I told Frank what the doctor said, and Frank told me I was exaggerating because I was lazy and didn't care about how his back felt.
(beat)
One day shortly after that, after a long time rubbing his back, my own was sore. And so I said "Your turn, and I want a half an hour because I always give you a half an hour, - what's fair is fair." And Frank said "I thought you gave me back rubs because you love me not because you expected something in return?" And I explained that I love him, but I also wanted something since I give so much. Then he told me I was just being selfish, and I needed to start trying to be a truly selfless person.
(beat)
And so I tried to be selfless for awhile, but the shooting pains in my arms, which he also refused to massage, were so unbearable that finally I figured it would just be easier to kill Frank than continue trying to be selfless. And I know I should have just left, or something, but the apartment was so

nice and why should I be the one to give it up? I'm the one who found it in the first place. And I suppose even then, there were other ways to handle things, but I couldn't think of any at the time. Killing him was the best I could come up with.

(beat)

Frank loved taking pictures. He had a camera on a timer when it happened. I was trying to make a turducken for him. He said he wanted to catch me doing something stupid.

(Holds up roll of film)

He succeeded. The real problem with me and Frank was, I think, my inability to be assertive. To assert myself. I mean, had I just asserted my right to back rubs, and to my arms, and to my apartment *which I found,* then maybe Frank would have respected my needs and I wouldn't have felt that killing him was the only option available to me.

(beat)

I think I fluctuate between being too passive and too aggressive when what I really need is to find some middle ground between the two.

(TRENT appears in the background, speaking to the audience)

TRENT

Everyone in town calls Lacey Mathews a black widow, because all of the men she becomes involved with end up dying

LACEY

After Frank, I had a series of relationships which ended badly.

TRENT

I always thought that Lacey just hadn't met the right guy yet: I knew if given a chance, I could turn her around.

LACEY

Lately I've been wondering where it all went wrong. It's not like I wanted to become a serial…dater.

TRENT

I'd often dreamt of finding the sweet, sensitive woman I knew was buried within. Then suddenly it looked like I would be given my chance to do just that.

LACEY

Before I killed my therapist, he came up with a great idea: why not develop this film and take a good hard look at my anger? Maybe then I could learn to channel all my pent up energy in healthier ways – like for origami! So I took my film to the Quickie Mart. They do one hour developing.

(Lacey hands Trent the film)

TRENT

As if she sensed the long unspoken chemistry between us, she entrusted me with material so sensitive...like she was calling out to me, reaching out to a soul she knew could understand her.

LACEY

I assumed that killing the store clerk at the Quickie Mart would be an unfortunate necessity, a mild setback on my road to self discovery and inner healing.

(Trent pockets the film and pull out a stack of photos, he begins looking through   them).

TRENT

It was like, with this photographic confession she was calling out to me, to rescue her from herself.

LACEY

The clerk is this sweet dorky little man whom I'd known since high school, but for the life of me I couldn't remember his name? I kept thinking, what is it? Dan, or something?

TRENT

My name's Trent by the way: Hi.

LACEY
I paced outside the store an hour. Then I went in to pick up my film.

(Lacey crosses to the door to the Quickie Mart, and enters)

LACEY
Hi. Did you develop my film yet?

TRENT
I know everything, Lacey. We can be together at last.

LACEY
What are you talking about, Dan?   Give me my pictures.

TRENT
They're beautiful.

LACEY
What are you sick? They're of a man getting stabbed.

TRENT
(Star struck)
Not just getting stabbed...getting stabbed <u>by you</u>.

LACEY
Well. Sorry. You're a witness. I have to kill you now, Dan.

TRENT
It's Trent.

LACEY
I thought it was Dan.

TRENT
Killing me isn't necessary.

LACEY

My body is my weapon.
>(She does the karate kid crane and kick, then ends
with a karate stance)
Prepare to die.
>(She edges toward Trent)

TRENT

I was scared, naturally. But I was able to think on my feet.
*Wait, Lacey. This goes against all that you are. Remember
your speech at graduation?*

LACEY

Frank and I met in high school – he thought it would be a
funny joke to convince me I was valedictorian.

TRENT

The entire student council had played along with it.

LACEY

I've always been gullible, it's a weakness.

TRENT

I thought her speech was beautiful. *I remember it Lacey:
"We must go out and live honest, upright lives – lives of our
own unique vision, infused with the goodness and grace of
our spirit –*

TRENT AND LACEY

*"Go class of 1995 – go out into that vast world and do
something great – make life better for all of us."*

>(She's about to karate chop him, she stops to say…)

LACEY

Wow, you memorized that?

TRENT

I've memorized a lot of things about you.

LACEY

You have a - a crush?

TRENT

Remember that time you wanted to make your boyfriend jealous, so you threw me against the locker and rammed your tongue down my throat as he walked by?

LACEY

Vaguely.

TRENT

I *remember it like it was yesterday. Lacey, I think we can build something special here – you and me. What do you say? Can we give it a shot?*

LACEY

Well…okay, maybe. Something about him intrigued me. And also I thought, if I can't make it work with a piece of milquetoast like this, then I really am doomed.

TRENT

Lacey, I think all relationships start with a foundation of trust. I learned this trust exercise in my AA meetings. Stand, there
            (He positions her)
You close your eyes. Now, let yourself fall. Believe…I'll catch you. Go ahead. Believe.

LACEY

And for the first time, maybe ever, I did.
            (Lacey lets herself fall, Trent catches her).
You – you caught me.

TRENT

I always will.   I was confident that this time, with me by her side, Lacey would make it work.   Especially since I was a student of Yoda Yoga…it's an intensely spiritual form of yoga studied by Jedi masters like myself….

(Both take on Yoga postures. Trent instructs, changing positions, Lacey mirrors   him)

TRENT (cont.)
A physical discipline, this is. Spiritual strength, it brings. Love, the same is. Positions of love, we put ourselves in. Through disciplined practice, does love grow strong. The feeling of love, passive and fleeting it is. The practice of love, active and enduring it is. This truth, as ancient and timeless as Yoda himself. Yodaste (pronounced like Namaste)

LACEY
Yodaste. And so it began. I decided it would be better to have the relationship away from my apartment since that'd always been a sore point with me…

TRENT
I decided, that since I lived with my mom, there would only be one other place we could comfortably be together…given my meager financial means.

LACEY
And so we took up a secret residence in the Quickie Mart nights.

TRENT
And began our affair, our happy life together.
(Trent flips the sign in the window, so it says "closed."
They carry a couch in and sit or lay on it together).
We began, like many couples, unloading baggage from previous relationships.

LACEY

And then there was my third late boyfriend. He just snored something awful. I said to him "Please just wear a breath right strip." He got irate "you're saying I'm breathing wrong?" That's when he began eating ten cans of beans in bed nightly.

TRENT

No!

LACEY

It was like trying to sleep beside a horn section. Two years of that and his constant marriage proposals ending in "syeeek!"and I had enough. "Get out of my apartment" I screamed, (suddenly timid) *"or marry me, please" "Ok" he said "I'll marry you." "Really?" I said. "Sure" he said. Then he put on a breath right strip and put down the can opener. Was I dreaming? He said "lie back" I did. I felt his hands caressing my hair. He began to sing quietly to me. I couldn't make out the words – but his voice was like butter and I began to drift off.*

TRENT

Nice.

LACEY

It was. Until I made out the lyrics to his little lullaby "Beans, beans the musical fruit, the more I eat the more I toot!" I opened my eyes and he had this toothy grin. He was holding a finger out to me "pull it" he said. Something in me died right there. Later that night he died. Asphyxiation by pillow. The police blamed it on his sleep apnea. 60 Minutes did a story about what happened.

TRENT

Not "When Crib Death Strikes the King Sized Bed"?

LACEY

Yes! You saw that?

TRENT

Hard hitting stuff.

LACEY

*Mm hm. Anyway, that's some of the baggage from my
previous relationships. Honey, you don't want to hear it all.*

    (pause)

TRENT

*I haven't had any previous relationships. Well, I had a hand
job once...sort of.*
    (awkward pause)
So...what about the guy getting killed in the photos...?

LACEY

I wasn't ready to talk about Frank.

TRENT

She would tell me about him later.

LACEY

There just were too many painful memories.

TRENT

Like the time Frank took her to his friend's costume party.

LACEY

He was dressed as an oak tree and I was dressed as a bear
rug. His suggestion.

TRENT

She drove.

LACEY

As usual he sat in the back seat and had me drop him off at
the door and find parking.

TRENT

She enters the party.

                         LACEY
Everyone goes quiet and stares.

                         TRENT
Frank didn't tell Lacey his friend worked for PETA.

                         LACEY
People started yelling at me

                         TRENT
"how inappropriate" "how dare you"

                         LACEY
(Very upset at being called this) "animal killer."

                         TRENT
A soy burger soars through the air, hitting her in the face.

                         LACEY
(As if she's been hit) Ouch. I make out a tree moving
through the crowd. It emerges snapping pictures. Between
the flash of the camera and the soy burger, I'm blind, but I
hear this shriek of delight: Frank's voice calling out -

                         TRENT
"APRIL FOOLS!" The weird thing about the whole story is
it wasn't April.

                         LACEY
Frank did that sort of thing year round. It didn't matter when
it was he'd always call out "April Fools!"

                         TRENT
And snap pictures of her looking mortified.

                         LACEY
Frank loved taking pictures.

                              TRENT
But she didn't tell me this at first.

                              LACEY
I just said: *I'm not ready to talk about the man in the photos.*

                              TRENT
I understand, darling.   She eventually began to open up
about him. The first time she mentioned his name was while
we were making love.

                              LACEY
Don't ruin it for them, we're getting there.   Like all
relatively new relationships, this one started out...

                              TRENT
...rife with sexual tension...

                              LACEY
...in short, very awkward...*I think a lot of men have trouble
seeing past my breasts to my personality.*

                              TRENT
Not me.

                              LACEY
You're finding not looking down...difficult. Aren't you?

                              TRENT
Very.

                              LACEY
Go ahead. Look at them.

                              TRENT
Thank you.

LACEY

Are you done yet?

TRENT

Hold on.

LACEY

Get it out of your system.

TRENT

Okay.

LACEY

Okay?

TRENT

(Looking up at her) *Yeah. No.* (Looks back down)

LACEY

Soon, however, we progressed to deeper levels of intimacy.

TRENT

Who's my sugar plum?

LACEY

I'm your sugar plum!

TRENT

Who's my sugar plum?

LACEY

I'm your sugar plum!

TRENT

Sugar…plum.

LACEY

Say it again!

                    TRENT
Sugar plum.

                    LACEY
Again!

                    TRENT
SUGAR PLUMMMMMM!

              LACEY AND TRENT
          (They begin passionately making out)
Oh Oh oh oh oh
          (They fall behind the couch)
oh oh oh

                    TRENT
oh oh OH –

                    LACEY
Oh FRANK!

                    TRENT
Frank?

                    LACEY
The man in the photos.

                    TRENT
Oh!

              LACEY AND TRENT
Oh...oh...oh...oh....

                    TRENT
OHHHHHHHHHHH YEEEEAAAAAAAAH
          (He appears from behind the couch)
That was great!

LACEY
(Appears from behind the couch, not satisfied at all)
Yeah.

TRENT
I feel so close to you.

LACEY
Uh huh.

TRENT
*Like I could tell you anything. Even reveal my weaknesses
and I'd be safe.*

LACEY
You are safe.

TRENT
*Then it's fine to tell you I am the most lactose intolerant
person you've ever met. The slightest drop of milk and I'm a
goner.*

LACEY
If you drink it?

TRENT
If I even touch it. Poof. Dead. After several weeks of new
relationship bliss…things started to go…a little sour…

LACEY
Slowly, the rose colored glasses of infatuation lost their tint,
and reality once again came into focus. *Trent, why can't you
get a better job so we don't have to be squatters at the
Quickie Mart?*

TRENT
What? Now you don't like it here?

LACEY

No.

TRENT

We're king and queen of the world here, Lacey.

LACEY

Maybe I want more from life!

TRENT

But we can drink all the 7up we want here!

LACEY

I don't want any more 7up.

TRENT

What about Sprite?

LACEY

It's the same goddamned thing.

TRENT

You used to be able to taste the difference.

LACEY

I just pretended to.
            (Trent looks crushed)
Weeks passed...I tried to stick it out. I tried to calm my
anger, to do one of those little origami birds. But it just came
out all mangled. I tried to practice Yoda's discipline of love.

(Trent and Lacey take on Yoda Yoga poses together)

TRENT

*Yoda teaches: to feel love, easy it is. To hold onto love -
another story that is.* And even the best of us are susceptible
to the dark side.

LACEY

I think we need to re-establish trust in our relationship. Let's do that trust relationship exercise of yours.

TRENT

You're right, let's do it. I love you. We can get us back.

LACEY

I love you too.

TRENT

I read in Cosmo that lasting love is a process of falling for your mate, not once but over and over again. *Fall for me again, Lacey.*

LACEY

I'm scared.

TRENT

You're safe with me. Go ahead and fall.

(Lacey gets in position and closes her eyes. Trent stands ready to catch her).

TRENT

Ready?

LACEY

Ready!

(Phone rings. Trent goes to get it. He picks it up.)

TRENT

Hello?
    (Lacey FALLS flat on her back— mats are needed for this show)
Mmm hmm, mmm hmm. No, big daddy can't come visit you now, not now my sugar puff, big daddy's girlfriend is home.
    (Trent hangs up.)

LACEY

*Now you have a mistress!? When did you get a mistress?
Who is she? I want to know!? Is it one of my friends?*

TRENT

I'm not having an affair.

LACEY

Yes you are. You called her your sugar puff!

TRENT

No I didn't.

LACEY

I heard you!

TRENT

*I was talking about…cookies. Girl scout cookies. They sell
something called sugar puffs now.*

LACEY

No they don't.

TRENT

Yes they do! You just never heard of them you nitwit.

LACEY

Oh.

TRENT

*Now look, you've gone and made me angry. And you know
how the guy who works in the pharmacy section said I'm
supposed to watch my blood pressure. You're so selfish, all
you're ever worried about is whether or not I cheated on you.
Why don't you worry about how I feel for a change before
you go accusing me! Don't you love me?*

LACEY

Yes.

TRENT

There now. Everything's fine between us. Get me a bottle of water, would you?

LACEY

Why can't you get it, you're right there.

TRENT

Please.

LACEY

Alright sweetheart.
        (She crosses the entire room to hand him a water that was sitting right next to   him).
Honey? Why don't you call me your sugar plum, anymore?

TRENT

Well I realized…a sugar plum…it's really just…a prune.

LACEY

And then it hit me. I was being too passive again. Hiding my true feelings. And I realized: It was time to kill Trent and start over with someone new, or perhaps give up on love altogether.
(Lacey grabs a bottle of milk and begins edging toward Trent with it)

TRENT

Lacey, what are you doing? You know I have a deathly allergy!!!! Come on now, be reasonable.

LACEY

I don't feel reasonable.

TRENT

Aha!!!!
        (Trent pulls out a camera and starts taking pictures)
APRIL FOOLS!!!! I don't have an allergy…and Frank.

LACEY

No! No!!!!

TRENT

Frank's not dead. You think that was a real knife you used on him in those pictures? You're so gullible. It was a retracting plastic blade and he used blood pellets. Ahahahaha. He's been planning this whole thing for years. This whole time, I've been acting, ever since the trust exercise, it's all been an act, our whole affair. Yeah Frank'll love these pictures, he got you again. Just like he got you at high school graduation and at the costume party. You're a born sucker Lacey!!!!

LACEY

And then I ran out, crying.

TRENT

Frank is dead, to clear that up for you, I just lied to her to save my ass. I gave her some time to calm down, then I went and looked for her.

LACEY

Letting the anger roll off was good. He was the first man I grew to hate and didn't kill. Then, after a time, he came to me, in my apartment. He was so sweet and apologetic, and he gave me this – this nice little book on Origami.

TRENT

And I stay there with her, at her *apartment*, but I keep my stuff at the Quickie Mart, so she doesn't feel like I'm encroaching on her space.

LACEY

And he promised to stop seeing sugar puff.

TRENT

And it's not perfect. Not like I thought it would be.

                    LACEY
And I still want to kill him sometimes.

                    TRENT
But we've worked out a comfortable life for two. And I call
her sugar plum.

                    LACEY
Yes, we work it out everyday.

                    TRENT
And that's enough for us.

                    LACEY
Day…

                    TRENT
By day…

                    LACEY
By day.

        (Lacey turns to Trent and hands him a small, neatly
folded origami bird. They smile uneasily at each other. Fade
to black)

                    FIN

Lacey's Last Chance

A Play in Ten Minutes

by

Gabriel Davis

gabriel@alumni.cmu.edu
www.gabrielbdavis.com

Characters

Lacey
In her mid twenties

Trent
In his mid twenties

Place

An empty space which
becomes a Quickie Mart

Time

The Present

(The action fluctuates between audience address and standard scene work)

(LACEY enters a bare stage, holding a mannequin, she places the mannequin down, and addresses the audience)

LACEY

My father was a wonderful man who waited on me hand and foot when I was a child. Mother used to jokingly call him "the slave." When I grew up, I expected to find a husband as loving and selfless as my father. Instead I found Frank.

(Lacey looks at the mannequin)

I would always give Frank thirty minute back rubs, which he always asked for. He'd never give me back rubs unless I begged, and then only for thirty seconds. One time, I broke both my arms and they were put in casts. Despite this I continued with Frank's back rubs. The doctor warned me that if I continued using the muscles in my arms that way, I would permanently damage them and have unbearable shooting pains for the rest of my life. I told Frank what the doctor said. And Frank said:

(Lacey stands behind the mannequin, creating Frank's expressive arm movements and voice)

"Lacey, you're exaggerating because you're Lazy and you don't care about how my back feels. You're just being selfish, and you need to start trying to be a truly selfless person."

(beat)

And so I tried to be selfless for awhile, I rubbed him—

(She tries to rub him)

But the shooting pains in my arms were so unbearable that finally I figured it would just be easier to kill Frank—

(LACEY knocks mannequin over)

—than continue trying to be selfless. And I know I should have just left, or something, but the apartment was so nice and why should I be the one to give it up? I'm the one who found it in the first place. And I suppose even then, there

were other ways to handle things, but I couldn't think of any at the time. Killing him was the best I could come up with.
(beat)
The real problem was, I think, my inability to be assertive.
To assert myself.
(beat)
I think I fluctuate between being too passive and too aggressive when what I really need is to find some middle ground between the two.

(TRENT appears in the background, speaking to the audience)

TRENT
Everyone in town calls Lacey Mathews a black widow, because all of the men she becomes involved with end up dying.

LACEY
After Frank, I had a series of relationships which inevitably didn't work out.

TRENT
I always thought that Lacey just hadn't met the right guy yet: I knew if given a chance, I could turn her around.

LACEY
My last boyfriend, Jack, was a photographer. He died, well, he died on account of being an asshole which caused me to kill him. The difference with this, um, breakup was I had a chance to learn, to change. See, Jack had a camera on a timer which caught the whole messy thing on film, frame by frame.

TRENT
I'd often dreamed of finding the sweet, sensitive woman I knew was buried within. Then suddenly it looked like I would be given my chance to do just that.

LACEY

And I thought. Lacey, you should use this photo opportunity
for self examination. Maybe if I could get a good objective
look at my anger, I could learn to use it in healthier ways,
like for origami. And so I took the film to the local Quickie
Mart, which also did one hour developing.

TRENT

As if she sensed the long unspoken chemistry between us,
she entrusted me with material so sensitive…like she was
calling out to me, reaching out to a soul she knew could
understand her.

LACEY

I assumed that killing the store clerk at the Quickie Mart
would be an unfortunate necessity, a mild setback on my
road to self discovery and inner healing.

TRENT

It was like, with this photographic confession she was calling
out to me, to rescue her from herself.

LACEY

The clerk is this sweet dorky little man whom I'd known
since high school, but for the life of me I couldn't remember
his name? I kept thinking, what is it? Dan, or something?

TRENT

My name's Trent by the way: Hi.

LACEY

I waited an hour. Then I went to pick up my film.

        (Lacey crosses to the door to the Quickie Mart, and
enters)

LACEY

Hi. Did you develop my film yet?

TRENT

I know everything, Lacey. We can be together at last.

LACEY

What are you talking about, Dan?   Give me my pictures.

TRENT

They're beautiful.

LACEY

What are you sick? They're of a man getting stabbed.

TRENT

Not just getting stabbed…getting stabbed by you.

LACEY

Well. Sorry. You're a witness. I have to kill you now, Dan.

TRENT

It's Trent.

LACEY

I thought it was Dan.

TRENT

Killing me isn't necessary.

LACEY

My body is my weapon.
        (She does the karate kid crane and kick, then ends
with a karate stance).
Prepare to die.
        (She edges toward Trent).

TRENT

I was scared, naturally. But I was able to think on my feet.
Wait, Lacey. This goes against all that you are. Remember
your speech at graduation?

LACEY

Frank had thought it would be a funny joke to convince me I
was valedictorian.

TRENT
Even the principal had played along with it.

LACEY
I've always been gullible, it's a weakness.

TRENT
But her speech was beautiful. Like her. I remember it
Lacey: "We must go out and live honest, upright lives –
lives of our own unique vision, infused with the goodness
and grace of our spirit –

TRENT AND LACEY
"Go class of 1994 – go out into that vast world and do
something great – make life better for all of us."

(She's about to karate chop him, she stops to say…)

LACEY
Wow, you memorized that?

TRENT
I've memorized a lot of things about you.

LACEY
You have a - a crush?

TRENT
Remember that time you wanted to make Frank jealous, so
you threw me against the locker and rammed your tongue
down my throat as he walked by?

LACEY
Vaguely.

TRENT

I remember it like it was yesterday. Lacey, I think we could build something special here – you and me. What do you say? Can we give it a shot?

LACEY
Well…okay, maybe. Something about him intrigued me. And also I thought, if I can't make it work with a piece of milk-toast like this, then I really am doomed.

TRENT
Lacey, I think all relationships start with a foundation of trust. I learned this trust exercise at community college over the summer. Stand, there (he positions her) You close your eyes. Now, let yourself fall. Believe…I'll catch you. Go ahead. Believe.

LACEY
And for the first time, maybe ever, I did.
        (Lacey lets herself fall, Trent catches her).
You – you caught me.

TRENT
I always will.   I was confident that this time, with me by her side, Lacey would make it work.

LACEY
And so it began. I decided it would be better to have the relationship away from my apartment since that'd always been a sore point with me…

TRENT
I decided, that since I lived with my mom, there would only be one other place we could comfortably be together…given my meager financial means.

LACEY
And so we took up a secret residence in the Quickie Mart nights.

TRENT

And began our affair, our happy life together.
(They carry a couch in. Lacey sits on Trent's lap).
We began, like most couples, unloading baggage from
previous relationships.

LACEY

…and so that's the deal with Frank. Then there was Stew, he
snored so I smothered him. And Andy, he was a wishy-
washy dinner decider, so I bumped him into a Mack Truck.
And so that's it, my baggage from previous relationships.

(pause)

TRENT

I haven't had any previous relationships. Well, I had a hand
job once…sort of.
        (Lacey abruptly moves off of Trent)
So…you didn't say anything about Jack.

LACEY

Truthfully, I didn't want to. Jack was probably the worst of
the men I dated. He was always playing tricks on me and
then screaming out "APRIL FOOLS!" even when it wasn't
April. He did it year round. And being a photographer, he
always caught whatever prank it was on film.

TRENT

One time he hired a bunch of friends to pretend to be
professors and students and sent her to a fake Rabbinical
school. They trained her as a Priest and then got her a job at
a synagogue.

LACEY

I wasn't Jewish by birth, how did I know they don't believe
in our lord and savior? Anyway, it wasn't fun to experience
and it wasn't fun to recount, so at the time I'd said: Trent I
don't want to talk about Jack, right now.

TRENT

I understand, darling.   She eventually told me the whole
thing, while we were making love actually, right before
climax, she whispered it in my ear.

LACEY

Don't ruin it for them, we're getting there.   Like all
relatively new relationships, this one started out...

TRENT

...rife with sexual tension...
        (Lacey drops something and picks it up. She catches
Trent checking her out)

LACEY

...in short, very awkward...
Soon, however, we progressed to deeper levels of intimacy.

TRENT

Who's my sugar plum?

LACEY

I'm your sugar plum!

TRENT

Who's my sugar plum?

LACEY

I'm your sugar plum!

TRENT

Sugar...plum.

LACEY

Say it again!

TRENT

Sugar plum.

LACEY

Again!

TRENT

SUGAR PLUMMMMMM!

LACEY AND TRENT
(they fall behind the couch together)
Oh Oh oh oh oh
(arms and legs begin flying up in a rhythmic
sequence)
oh oh oh

TRENT

oh oh OH so THAT'S the story about Jack.

LACEY AND TRENT

oh oh oh

TRENT

OHHHHHHHHHH YEEEEAAAAAAAAS
(He appears from behind the couch)
That was great!

LACEY
(She appears from behind the couch, not satisfied at
all)
Yeah.

TRENT

A secret about me: I've got a deathly allergy to chocolate
milk. A cup of the stuff could kill me.

LACEY

Remember that for later.

TRENT

Then…after several weeks of new relationship bliss…things
started to go…a little sour…

LACEY

Slowly, the rose colored glasses of infatuation lost their tint, and reality once again came into focus. Trent, why can't you get a better job so we don't have to be squatters at the Quickie Mart?

TRENT

What? Now you don't like it here? You don't like these cheese curls? Why don't you get a job?

LACEY

Weeks passed…I tried to stick it out. I practiced the discipline of love. It was hard…
I think we need to re-establish trust in our relationship. Let's do that trust exercise of yours.

TRENT

You're right, let's do it. I love you. We can get us back.

LACEY

Let's do it.

TRENT

Ready?

LACEY

Ready!

(They get into position. Trent, ready to catch her. Lacey, eyes closed, ready to fall. Phone rings. Trent goes to get it.)

TRENT

Hello?
    (LACEY FALLS flat on her back)
Mmm hmm, mmm hmm. No, big daddy can't come visit you now, not now my sugar puff, big daddy's girlfriend is home.
    (Trent hangs up.)

LACEY

Now you have a mistress!? When did you get a mistress?
Who is she? I want to know!? Is it one of my friends? Is it
Irene?

TRENT

I'm not having an affair.

LACEY

Yes you are. You called her your sugar puff!

TRENT

No I didn't.

LACEY

I heard you!

TRENT

I was talking about…cookies. Girl scout cookies. They sell
something called sugar puffs now.

LACEY

No they don't.

TRENT

Yes they do! You just never heard of them you nitwit.

LACEY

Oh.

TRENT

Now look, you've gone and made me angry. And you know
how the doctor said I'm supposed to watch my blood
pressure. You're so selfish, all you're ever worried about is
whether or not I cheated on you. Why don't you worry about
how I feel for a change before you go accusing me! Don't
you love me?

LACEY

Yes.

                    TRENT
There now. Everything's fine between us.

                    LACEY
Honey…why don't you call me Sugar Plum, anymore?

                    TRENT
Well I realized…a sugar plum…it's really just…a prune…

                    LACEY
And then it hit me. I was being too passive again. Hiding
my true feelings. And I realized: It was time to kill Trent
and start over with someone new, or perhaps give up on love
altogether.
(Lacey pantomime grabs a bottle of chocolate milk, points, to
audience)
Chocolate milk!
(She moves threateningly toward Trent, who sits on the
couch, oblivious. Suddenly Trent pantomimes holding up a
book)

                    TRENT
Oh by the way, I got you a book on origami.

                    LACEY
And then I realized, I didn't have to kill Trent!
        (beat)
I could fold paper!
        (She grabs the book, crying)
And then, I ran out crying.

                    TRENT
I felt bad about how I'd treated Lacey. So, I gave her some
time to calm down, or whatever, then I went and looked for
her.

                    LACEY

Letting the anger roll off was good. He was the first man I grew to hate and didn't kill. Then, after a time, he came to me, in my apartment.

TRENT

And I stay there with her, but I keep my stuff at the Quickie Mart, so she doesn't feel like I'm encroaching on her space.

LACEY

And he promised to stop seeing sugar puff.

TRENT

And it's not perfect. Not like I thought it would be.

LACEY

And I still want to kill him sometimes.

TRENT

But we've worked out a comfortable life for two. And I call her sugar plum.

LACEY

Yes, we work it out everyday.

TRENT

And that's enough for us.

LACEY

Day…

TRENT

By day…

LACEY

By day.
        (Lacey places a paper Origami Bird on Trent's hand.
Whispers)
Chirp, Chirp.

THE END

Printed in Great Britain
by Amazon